The Mystery Of
CARL WARK:
Peak District Fortress Or Folly?

by

Mick Savage

© Mick Savage 1999

Printed and published by:
ALD Design & Print
279 Sharrow Vale Road
Sheffield S11 8ZF

Telephone: (0114) 268 6269
E:mail: ald@printshop.demon.co.uk

ISBN 1-901587-06-1

First Published 1999

All rights reserved
No part of this publication may be reproduced, stored in a retrieval system or transmitted in any form or by any means, electronic, mechanical, photocopying, recording or otherwise, without prior written permission of the publisher.

All views and comments printed in this book are those of the author and should not be attributed to the publisher.

Front cover photograph by courtesy of Laurance Richardson. Rear cover aerial photograph by courtesy of English Heritage National Monuments Records, reference SK2681 FR12

Other titles in the series:	ISBN
Mi-Amigo - The Story of Sheffield's Flying Fortress - David Harvey	1-901587-00-2
Tales From a Peak District Bookshop - Mike Smith	1-901587-01-0
Tha' Don't Look Proper - Anne Hunt	1-901587-02-9
Shiny Sheff - The Story of Sheffield's Fighting Ships - Alistair Lofthouse	1-901587-03-7
Doug's War - An Erksome Business - Doug Sanderson	1-901587-04-5
The Dramatic Story of the Sheffield Flood - Peter Machan	1-901587-05-3

Coming Soon

Sheffield Then & Now - Alistair Lofthouse   1-901587-07-X

Contents

Please Note	iv
Preface	v
Acknowledgements	vi
Introduction	
The trouble with research: finding more questions than answers	1
An archaeological dilemma: what exactly is a hillfort?	7
A modest host to hundreds of visitors	9
Putting Carl Wark on the map	
The geography of the surrounding area	11
The living and the dead: Hathersage and Mam Tor	13
Roman influence: the fort at Brough and the network of roads	15
What can we see today?	17
The mystery of Caer's Chair	25
Conflict and Construction	
Population & prestige: climatic changes take effect	31
Fortress or folly: was Carl Wark really built for defence?	32
When exactly was the Iron Age?	34
Metalworking: an essential skill for the Iron Age	37
Where are the ghosts?	38
Making a living: everyday life and trade in the surrounding area	42
Searching for the origins of Carl Wark: archaeological finds in the area	45
Carl Wark resurrected: could there have been two phases of construction?	46
Unique features: the western rampart and entrance	48
The Celtic Tribes of Britain	
Turbulent times: the Roman invasion and its aftermath	53
Flight to fight: the Romans temporarily withdraw from the region	58
Could Carl Wark have been built with the consent of the Roman army?	59
The end of Roman civilisation: the beginning of the Dark Ages	60
More trouble: the Anglo-Saxon invasion	62
New kingdoms: Mercia, Northumbria and the coming of the Danes	63
Looking to the Future	
An archaeological challenge: what can be done to solve the mystery?	65
Chronology	68
Suggested Reading	69

Please Note

Carl Wark is a scheduled ancient monument and is protected by law. It is in an 'open access agreement' area of the Peak District National Park, so you are free to explore, but please remember that it is against the law to cause any damage or to use a metal detector in its vicinity. If you happen to come across any item which you think may be of archaeological interest you should carefully note the exact location of the find spot. If possible take a photograph of the object 'in situ' and then hand the object over to a responsible person at your local museum as soon as possible.

However tempting it may seem, you should never try to clean or restore anything you find as this could cause irreparable damage to the artefact. Cleaning must be left to expert conservationists.

Preface

Carl Wark could be compared to 'an immense blackened altar', exclaimed antiquarian Sidney Addy in 1893, pursuing a theme first introduced a hundred years earlier by Major Hayman Rooke, who was convinced that Carl Wark had been the Druids' seat of justice. It possessed 'a wild grandeur and solemn dignity not often witnessed in England', according to archaeologist Edward Trustram in 1911, writing in a more secular mood.

Could it be that we once had an innate ability to understand the purpose of these ancient monuments but, through the aeons of time, it has been lost? Perhaps it was slowly subdued by an evolving cultural consciousness involving the replacement of our monuments' true meaning by the imposition of religious alternatives, or merely lost through lack of interest. There are groups even today which believe they are in touch with mysterious forces emanating from the stones at places like Stonehenge and Avebury. However bizarre the idea may seem to the average person, there can be no doubt that for the people concerned these perceptions are very real.

There can be few mysteries deeper than the riddle of the ancient monument known as Carl Wark, because here we have a structure which has been described by archaeologists as 'unlike any other found in Northern England'.

This book will appeal to anyone who is interested in discovering the origins of the landscape in which we live and, in particular, who wishes to know a little more about the history and archaeology of a small and mysterious part of the northern Peak District.

Acknowledgements

I am particularly indebted to Dr. John Barnatt, enthusiastic ambassador for archaeology and Senior Survey Archaeologist for the Peak District National Park Authority. I put on record my appreciation of John's willingness to answer my questions, despite being engaged in excavations at Gardom's Edge, and especially for reading and correcting this manuscript. Also my thanks to Sara Donaghey - for her encouragement and advice; Brian Donaghey - for translating Rooke's 18th century writing; Sarah Whitely, South Yorkshire Archaeological Unit - for access to files and computerised information and enthusiastic advice; Sheffield University Library staff, Sheffield City Library Staff and Jennifer Tzavaras, National Monuments Record Centre, Swindon - for their patience in finding materials for me. Thanks also to the Hunter Archaeological Society for permission to reproduce illustrations from Hayman Rooke's notebooks.

Introduction

The trouble with research: finding more questions than answers

Why, even today, are so many people fascinated by our country's ancient and mysterious monuments, standing stones, magnificent hilltop fortresses and other remarkable reminders of the past which are to be found all over the British Isles? Interest seems to have increased during the past few years as reflected in the number of popular television programmes about archaeology which have sprung up. Of course on the one hand these ruins are direct, tangible reminders of our ancestry, yet on the other there is something else, something that goes far deeper. Something that instils a sense of wonder in us. Something which captures our imagination. Who could fail to be impressed by the spectacle of a midsummer solstice sun rising over the heel stone at Stonehenge, or thrilled by a chance encounter with a lonely, mist shrouded cromlech somewhere in the Welsh mountains? Or fail to notice the feeling of power and security standing on the ramparts of a massive prehistoric fortress like Maiden Castle provides?

On the purely physical level these experiences also make us realise what a truly awesome enterprise building something so massive with primitive methods must have entailed. Why should our ancestors have undertaken such backbreaking endeavours? What were their motives? These are very difficult, if not impossible questions to answer, for these ancient and mysterious monuments share a deeply elusive paradox: although a great deal is known about them in the material sense, very little is understood about their original purpose or intention.

How can there be such a lack of understanding in this age of scientific discovery, of space exploration and quantum physics? The simple fact is that ancient monuments, erected before the advent of writing, can only bear mute testimony to our long forgotten past, so that the process of getting them to speak out is nowhere near as straightforward as it may seem. Like the dark depths of the oceans, we have so far only explored a fraction of what exists and we know even less about why it exists. So although by and large the vast majority of ancient monuments in Britain have been exhaustively described, measured and to some extent analysed, very often they have refused to yield their innermost secrets - their true purpose, despite the lifelong efforts of many eminent archaeologists and patient historians.

Through painstaking detailed excavation and interpretation, archaeologists can discover with increasing scientific accuracy and sophistication factual information, such as the chronology of a monument's construction phases, the sources of the materials used by its builders, the specialist techniques needed to manufacture artefacts like axes, shovels and so on, but still cannot say with certainty enough what the true purpose of many of our ancient monuments was - beyond offering well rehearsed ritualistic theories or far less convincing astronomical explanations.

To further complicate matters, stone monuments have existed for so many centuries that they have probably changed their purpose and significance through the long passage of time as succeeding generations interpreted or used them in ways which met their own needs. It is hardly surprising that in recent years we have seen the emergence of a new breed of 'time-detective', confident that they can bypass the traditionally laborious work of the archaeologists and solve the riddle of the stones by alternative means. But of course these self-styled earth-mystery investigators, enthusiastically equipped with dowsing rods and propounding alternative theories about ley lines and lost mystical powers, still struggle to find solutions, not knowing whether or not they are even asking the right questions.

In all this activity one should not lose sight of the possibility that some of the standing stones, hilltop constructions and other monuments to organised prehistoric labour on a massive scale may not have had any practical function at all! It could be that their raison d'être was nothing more mysterious than to be marvelled at! This is not such an unbelievable proposition when one considers modern examples of human endeavour (or folly!) like the massive steel angel erected on a hilltop overlooking the motorway at Gateshead in 1998.

How best then can we approach this thorny problem of interpretation? Well first of all it would be a mistake to think that each of these longlasting ruins stand alone. They are an integral part of a wholly human-made landscape, a landscape which is not as natural as it so often seems - and one of the reasons why the monuments seem to fit into the countryside so well. For the truth is that the apparently natural features of the British Isles have been shaped relentlessly by human occupation ever since the ice sheets retreated for the last time, although the evidence for this fact can be quite difficult to detect, particularly by the untrained eye. The relationship between a monument and its surrounding landscape is a complex equation which, if we can unravel it, may eventually lead to an understanding of what the people who built it had in mind at the time.

When beginning any research into the history of an ancient monument one obvious avenue of enquiry is to study the reports produced by archaeologists who have excavated the site. Most disappointingly, the results of the only known 'dig' at Carl Wark (by F. G. Simpson in 1950) were never published, so whatever information there was has been lost.

Only a brief reference to Simpson's small scale excavation survives within a report compiled a year later by another archaeologist, C. M. Piggott, who had taken an earlier interest in Carl Wark. Interestingly, Piggott's views about the origins of Carl Wark went directly against popular belief. He declared quite unequivocally that 'students of Iron Age forts in the highland zone of Britain will immediately be aware that there is nothing familiar in the defensive structure' of Carl Wark. It was a Dark Age construction, whereas most archaeologists were convinced that Carl Wark belonged to a much earlier period. It was an Iron Age hillfort.

Another archaeologist, Edward Trustram, writing in the Derbyshire Archaeological Journal for 1911 had also believed that Carl Wark was unique, but unlike Piggott he was convinced that it was the 'earliest and most interesting example in England of a fort defended by a stone wall'.

Because of these conflicting opinions and despite Piggott's strongly argued point of view, my initial efforts were concentrated on the popular view that Carl Wark was built during the Iron Age period. Eventually though, as Piggott had predicted the investigation widened enormously, well beyond the Iron Age and even later than Piggott's favoured Dark Ages.

How is this type of research carried out? Firstly, all the available evidence of the various archaeological finds in the locality has to be collated - a process known as 'desk-top archaeology'. Then, in the case of Carl Wark, various distinguished archaeologists' opinions concerning the continuity of occupation of 'hillforts' was studied, from which it became quite clear that Carl Wark's history may extend back much further in time than Piggott's Dark Ages - at least as far back as the Bronze Age.

Then in an exciting development, new theories about hilltop sites in the Peak District were published which seemed to be highly relevant to an ancient monument like Carl Wark, effectively taking the possible origins of the historic site even further back in time, as far as the Neolithic period.

In particular these new discoveries make it possible to reconsider Edward Trustram's early twentieth-century hypothesis of how the stone rampart came to be built. He believed that as the geology of Carl Wark had prevented its builders from digging a ditch and throwing up an earth rampart, the wealth of freely available rocks lying all around triggered the idea of building a stone wall, which would compensate for the lack of a ditch. Trustram believed that Carl Wark's builders had 'independently originated the idea of a defensive wall of stone'. It remains a truly unique example of very early indigenous ingenuity, owing nothing to the Romans or anyone else for that matter.

Nevertheless, the conflicting opinions about the date at which Carl Wark's impressive western stone rampart was built ensured that the research had to be directed to those turbulent periods of our history later than the Iron Age. It became necessary to consider what life must have been like around Carl Wark during the oppressive period of Roman occupation and after, into the shadowy Dark Ages and the more accessible Anglo-Danish period.

One puzzle was a lack of information about the origin of the monument's name. Quite often a place name can assist with the dating of the time a monument was constructed and even the origins of its builders. A preliminary visit to the Sheffield City Liibrary's very helpful local history section drew an immediate blank! Undaunted, further visits were made, concentrating on reading antiquarian books about Hallamshire and Derbyshire (Carl Wark was originally in Derbyshire until the county boundary was changed). This strategy did eventually produce some plausible explanations about the name.

Next, the experienced staff at the National Monuments Record centre, although unable to provide much extra information about Carl Wark itself, did provide a great deal of information about surrounding sites and finds. Desktop archaeological investigation of this kind is both useful and fascinating, but can lead to distractions unless one is highly selective about what further information to seek. One aspect of desktop research like this was that there were references to fieldwork by individuals which when studied more closely, did not appear to be too reliable, particularly when others with more knowledge had dismissed them. There were also straightforward differences of opinion, some quite marked, about Carl Wark's age, its features and even its geology! Whilst none of this might seem directly relevant it did serve to indicate that nothing about Carl Wark was in any way cut and dried.

Despite the obvious value of academic or desktop research, fieldwork cannot be underestimated, particular when undertaken in the same location at different times of the year, if a fuller picture of the area being studied is to be achieved. For example fires on the moorland near to Carl Wark cleared the heather and bracken to reveal numerous cairns and barrows which were not previously apparent.

For my part, I have tried to present all the information I have obtained objectively, in such a way that the reader can properly consider all the evidence and then make up his or her own mind.

An archaeological dilemma: what exactly is a hillfort?

The term 'hillfort' was once unambiguous and more or less taken for granted, but serious doubts have been cast on that simple definition by a number of very distinguished archaeologists. Although some had meticulously categorised various monuments as hillforts over the years, others were questioning these preconceived ideas about their use and their origins. Forde-Johnston in a detailed account of 1,366 Iron Age forts classifies Carl Wark as a Group 11 inland promontory fort. He asserts that 'Carl Wark is a perfectly straightforward promontory fort.... By any account it must be included as an Iron Age fort'. Another expert, Dyer, defines a hillfort as 'any fortified site that is defended by one or more banks and ditches and encloses areas as widely varied as 0.1 ha. to 240 ha.' Hogg begins his index of British Hillforts with 'an enclosure with substantial defences, usually on high ground and probably built between 1000 BC and AD 700 but showing no sign of Roman influences.' Cunliffe in 'The Iron Age: Society and Hillforts', whilst discussing the history of hillforts, breaks new ground, favouring an hypothesis based on continuity of use through what he calls 'socio-religious association', rather than defensive physical occupation.

Perhaps more mundanely, Roman accounts describe an attack on a hillfort at Devil's Dyke, Wheathampstead, in which they observed that many cattle were found within the defences. So the vexed question of what exactly constitutes a hillfort remains an active debate which cannot be ignored.

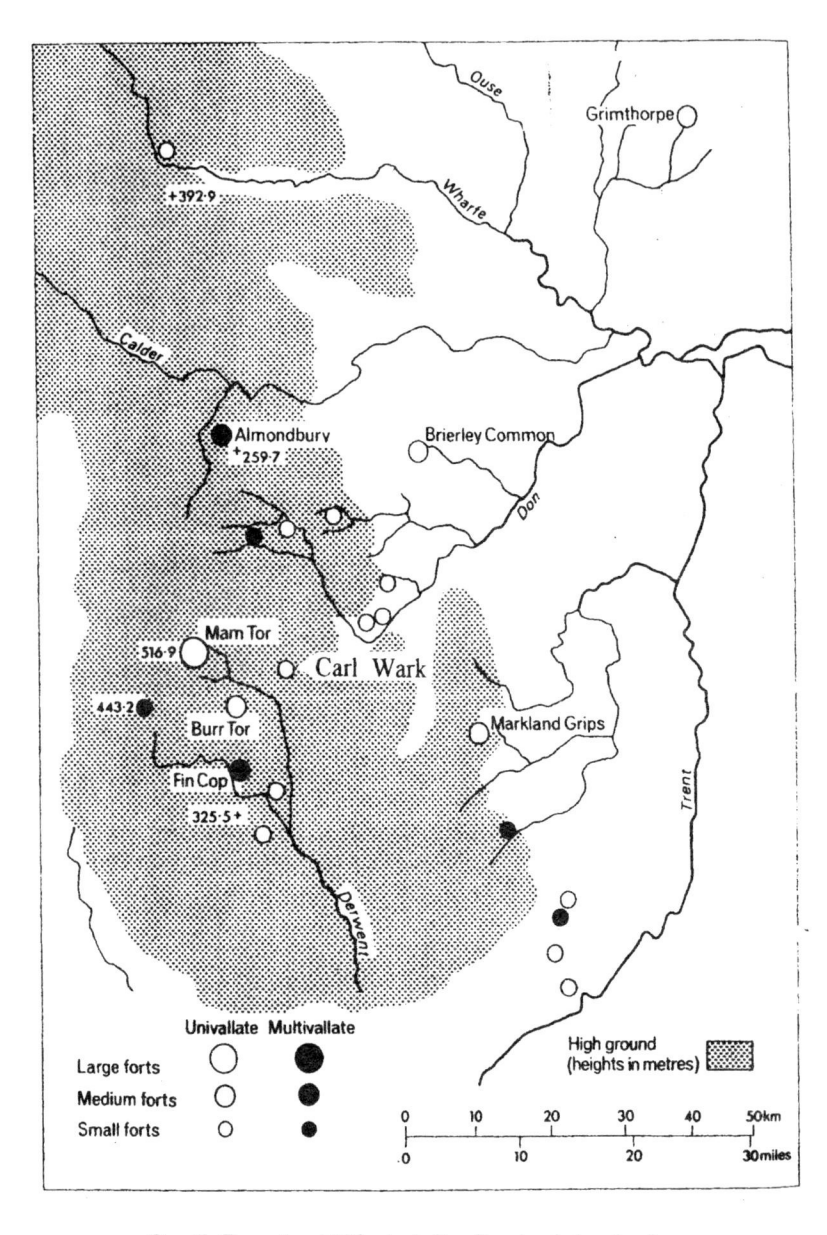

South Pennine Hillforts (after Forde-Johnston)

A modest host to hundreds of visitors

The natural rock outcrop on which Carl Wark sits is nowhere near as impressive as the neighbouring promontory of Higger Tor which towers over it. Nevertheless it is still a well-known landmark which hundreds of people visit every year. Some gather in family groups just to enjoy a picnic and perhaps a game of hide-and-seek amongst its huge boulders. Intrepid climbers with strong, chalk-white hands tackle the technical challenges presented by its sheer cliffs, unworried by any thought of the ghostly defenders who may once have guarded its rocky approaches. Some of the immense gritstone boulders which they swarm over today would, beyond the shadow of a doubt, have challenged any would-be attacker of long ago. But perhaps the majority of visitors who come to this lonely place, make the deceptively steep ascent purely out of curiosity. They want to know what Carl Wark is and why it's there. For its part the monument welcomes them, but it gives very little away.

At first sight one could be completely unaware that Carl Wark possesses any man-made features at all, or that there is a actually a huge amount of evidence of past human activity scattered across the surrounding landscape. As just one example, the area to the south of Carl Wark contains dozens of prehistoric field clearance cairns which are normally hidden by the tall bracken and tough heather. These ancient stone mounds only reveal themselves occasionally, perhaps when the cloak of vegetation is destroyed by fires or by the long shadows cast by late evening or early morning sunshine. And unless a visitor happens to approach Carl Wark through its steep and narrow artificial entrance, so that the massive western defensive wall is visible, it would be quite easy to mistake the man-made fortifications for the natural, chaotic jumble of giant millstone grit boulders so common to the tors in this part of the Peak District National Park and which give it its distinctive character.

There is a bronze plaque, erected on a stone pillar, immediately to the west of the fortification. This declares that Carl Wark is 'a 2000 - 2500 years old Iron Age hillfort', although an astute reader will notice that the inscription cautiously goes on to comment that it may have been re-fortified during the period of Roman occupation - a clear hint that little is officially known about the origins and history of this mysterious place.

There are only brief references to Carl Wark in a few guides for walkers or tourists describing the attractions of the Peak District National Park. Even those books aimed at the more serious, archaeologically minded reader or student, have little more than a brief description and some conjecture to offer. Some archaeologists have wisely described Carl Wark as an undated hillfort, but as already mentioned others favour placing it in the Iron Age period. This is based on the well established fact that the Iron Age was a time when hillforts proliferated in Britain. But we will see that the history of Carl Wark is far more interesting and complicated than that. Indeed as the evidence piles up, the Iron Age becomes the least likely building period of all.

Whatever your reasons for visiting Carl Wark are, it must be almost impossible to stand on this ancient monument's ramparts, perhaps gazing across to the western horizon and the massive neighbouring settlement atop the summit of Mam Tor, without being fascinated by its mysteries; without wondering about its origins and without wanting to turn back time, to ask someone 'who went to all the trouble of building this, and when, and why?' This book will help unravel some of Carl Wark's mysteries and suggest some answers to some so far unresolved questions. At the same time we shall be able to see a substantial piece of the history of this region unfold. It will enable us, through the monument's eyes, to take a journey into the past.

Putting Carl Wark on the Map

The geography of the surrounding area

It is probably no coincidence that Carl Wark does not dominate the moorland landscape, yet it has an unmistakably commanding presence. On certain days, depending on the weather, it seems benign, on other days it broods, even threatens. Sitting 370 metres above sea level on the bleak Hathersage Moor, one kilometre north of the A625 Sheffield to Hathersage road, it is today part of the extremely popular and magnificent Peak District National Park. Although it was once within the boundaries of Derbyshire, the area surrounding Carl Wark was transferred to the City of Sheffield in 1933. This means it is now in the county of South Yorkshire, formed in the 1970's. One wonders how many such territorial 'owners' it has had in its long lifetime before that latest expropriation?

Geologically, Carl Wark is a typical outcrop or 'tor' of a rock known locally as millstone grit. This is a coarse, pebbly, massive sandstone formed from an ancient sea bed which, unlike the surrounding shales, is erosion resistant. Sometimes this harder rock is referred to as 'Chatsworth' grit by geologists - a reference to the nearby Chatsworth Park estate, home of the Duke and Duchess of Devonshire.

So whilst the shale has been inexorably worn away by the elements through the aeons, the hard millstone grit has remained relatively untouched, the relentless forces of wind, rain and frost creating the strangely shaped, massive rock formations for which the region is so well known.

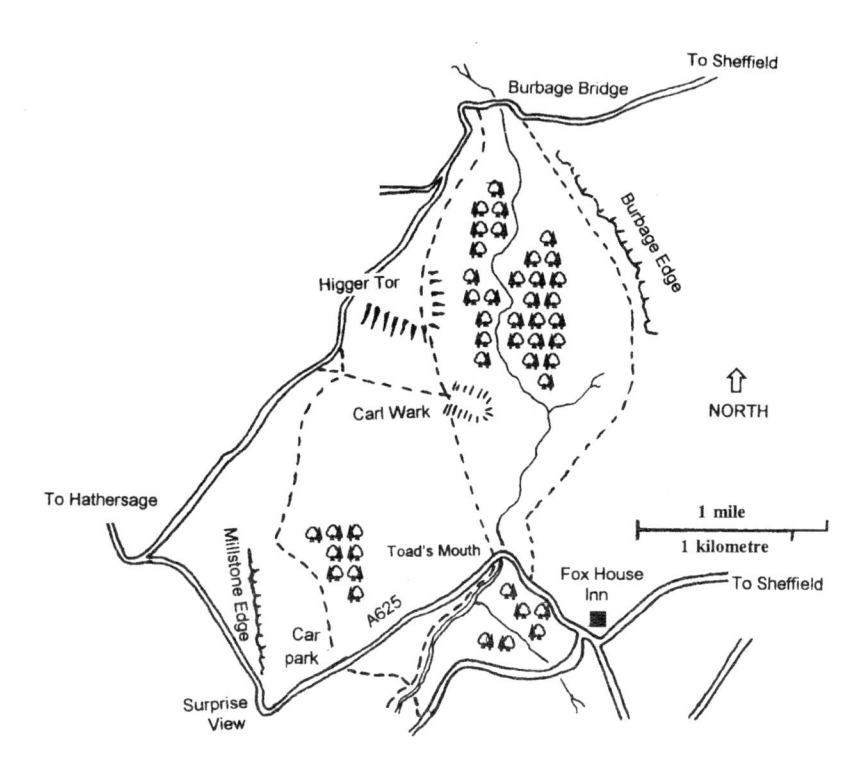

Footpaths around Carl Wark

Approximately five hundred metres to the north of Carl Wark and a good fifty metres higher is another gritstone outcrop, called Higger Tor, which at first glance seems far more suitable if one was in the business of choosing a fortified site two thousand years or so ago. Although the cliffs are imposing, closer inspection will reveal that Higger Tor levels off significantly to the north. As a result it does not provide anywhere near the same degree of natural all-round defence as Carl Wark, which is less exposed, both visually and perhaps equally importantly, climatically, than its more elevated neighbour.

Perhaps of even greater importance to ancient eyes searching the landscape for exactly the right place for their activities, is the fact that Higger Tor doesn't have the symmetry of Carl Wark.

To the east of Carl Wark, the rough moorland falls away quite steeply for about eighty metres to the tumbling, peaty waters of Burbage Brook, which is overlooked on the far side of this valley by a fine gritstone escarpment appropriately named Burbage Rocks, marking the western extremity of Burbage Moor, four hundred metres above sea level. These crags, known locally as Burbage Edge, with their warm south westerly aspect and easy access, have become increasingly popular with climbers.

To the west of Carl Wark the shallowest edge of the tor falls fairly gently for about thirty metres before it gradually rises up towards Millstone Edge. This prominent landmark, in reality once a huge quarry, is a Mecca for climbing enthusiasts from all over the country.

Interestingly, the 1875 Ordnance Survey map refers to Millstone Edge as Booths Edge, denoting its connection with the hamlet of Hathersage Booths, a short distance to the north west. Booth is a term commonly used in the Hope and Edale valleys to denote small, discrete hamlets, each of which had certain rights over the land, such as turbary (turf cutting). Millstone Edge probably gained its present colloquial name when tourists first began frequenting the area in significant numbers.

The living and the dead: Hathersage and Mam Tor

Below Millstone Edge, the busy little town of Hathersage is well patronised by tourists and local people alike. It boasts attractions as diverse as an open air heated swimming pool, cafés and restaurants, outdoor pursuits shops and activity centres, hotels and inns, a unique cutlery manufacturer, industrial training centre, camp sites and a youth hostel. But probably its most famous claim to fame is the grave of Robin Hood's giant ally, Little John, which can be easily found in the churchyard. Also worth a visit is the early Norman Camp Green ring work, adjacent to the medieval church of St. Michael. This is the largest ring work in North Derbyshire. Hathersage is the nearest town to Carl Wark and is a good example of an ancient settlement which is still very much alive today - exemplifying the concept of continuity of occupation in the landscape.

In complete contrast, looking out from Carl Wark's rampart over Hathersage towards the western horizon on a clear day one can see the abandoned settlement on the summit of Mam Tor. Geologically quite unlike Carl Wark, Mam Tor is an unstable shale hilltop. It is known locally as the Shivering Mountain, owing to the propensity for its shale to regularly fall away and for the hillsides below it to experience massive land slips akin to earthquakes. The main A625 Sheffield to Chapel En Le Frith road which once passed below the hill was closed to traffic long ago when the authorities finally gave up the hopeless battle against land slips which produced impassable chasms in the road's surface. Mam Tor's cliff edge can be extremely dangerous and has claimed the lives of several unsuspecting visitors over recent years.

Mam Tor is the site of a huge Bronze Age settlement which carbon-14 dating from two charcoal samples once suggested was first occupied somewhere between 1700 BC to 1000 BC. Unfortunately there are now doubts about the reliability of radiocarbon dates obtained in the 1960's when laboratory techniques were not as accurate as they are today. The substantial ramparts remain undated. Mam Tor is easily the largest defensive earthwork in the region and may well have been the focal point of activity of a society which occupied the Hope Valley and even farmed the Eastern Moors.

What would the original inhabitants of this defended hilltop settlement make if they would stand on its summit today, with its paved walkways and stone steps to combat the erosion caused by crowds of walkers, its groups of speeding mountain bikers, serenely floating parascenders and bird-like hang glider pilots?

Roman influence: the fort at Brough and the network of roads

Between Mam Tor and Carl Wark, at Brough-on-Noe, is the site of the Roman fort usually known as Navio, but sometimes referred to as 'Anavio'. Originally built between AD 75 and AD 120, there were in fact two distinctly different forts built here at various times. The original, perhaps hastily erected, wooden fort was replaced by a smaller but more substantial stone fort between AD 154-8 for reasons which will become apparent later.

Navio, like Ardotalia at modern-day Glossop, was probably built to protect the Romans' interest in the Peak District's lead mines, to protect east-west trade routes and of course, to enforce their occupation of the country. Like all forts built by the Roman army Navio was carefully positioned, in this case on a spur overlooking the River Noe to the north and east. The forts were part of an extensive network linked by fast military roads.

Over the years the river has eroded parts of Navio's remains away, but it is still possible to make out most of its outline. A public footpath runs through the middle of the site so it is relatively easy to visit. A few of the original stones remain in the field and in a few hidden places such as close by under a wooden footbridge. The road to Buxton still runs past the fort, passing through Bradwell village, even today raised above the surrounding land on the original Roman

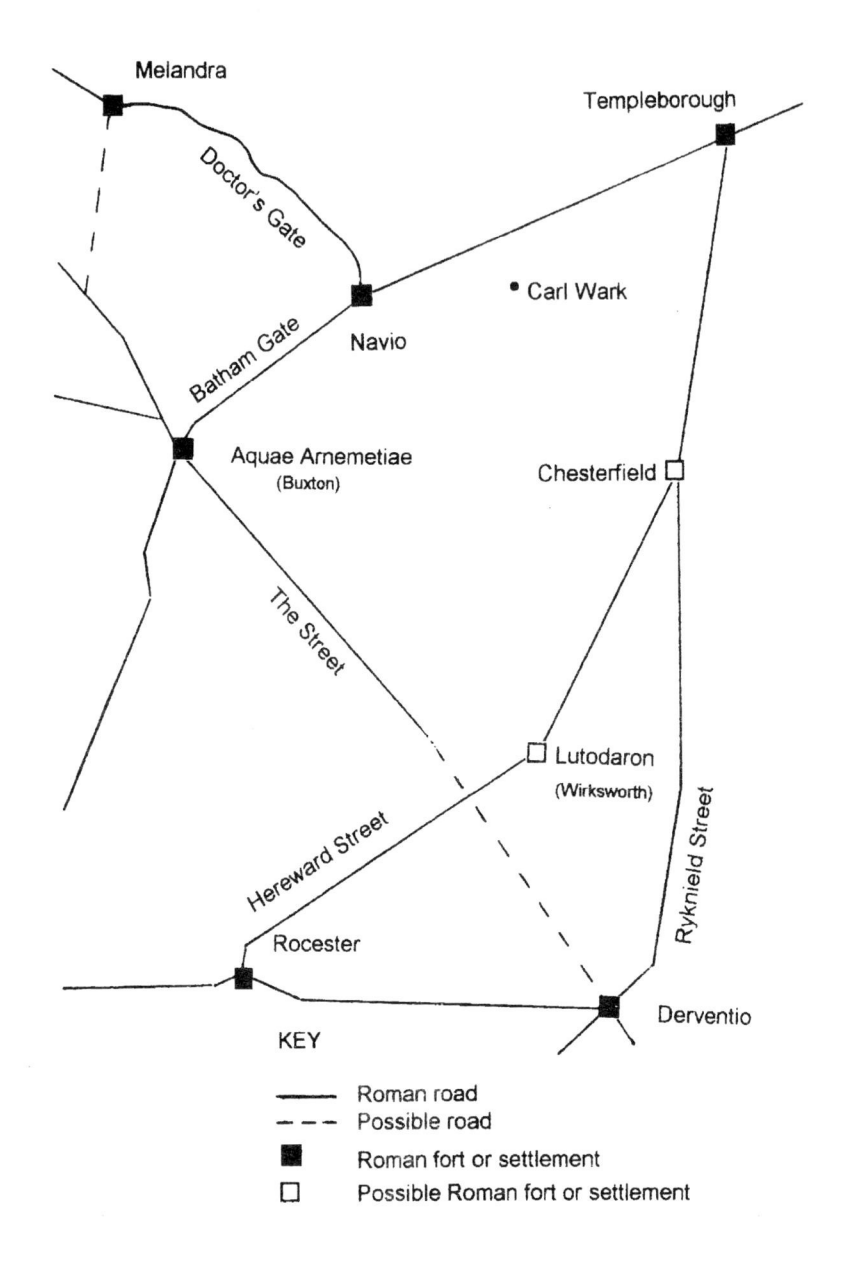

Network of Roman roads and forts around Carl Wark

causeway or agger. Buxton, with its naturally warm mineral springs, is still a very popular place for tourists to visit. In Roman times it was a spa known as Aquae Arnametiae - named after the Celtic goddess Arnametia. The present-day well dressing ceremonies which take place in the summer throughout Derbyshire are probably relics of the Celts' worship of vital water supplies.

Although another Roman road could be logically expected to have connected Navio to the larger fort at Templeborough, east of Sheffield and to Chesterfield (Cesterfelda - the field by the fort), its exact route is still not known and speculation about the course of the road abounds. For example, a track over Stanage Edge, known as Long Causeway, which incidentally passes about three kilometres to the north of Carl Wark is erroneously believed by a great number of local people to be the Roman road between Navio and Templeborough, but it is indisputably eighteenth century in origin. Another track believed by some to be the 'lost road' runs roughly eastwards away from Navio, cutting deeply into the hillside overlooking the River Noe and the road between Hope and Bamford, but recent excavation has shown this track to be much later than the Roman period and probably no older than post-medieval.

What can we see today?

Carl Wark's 'defences' utilise and enhance the natural features of a gritstone tor to enclose an almost oblong area of just over three quarters of a hectare (2 acres). Basically the site has three main features: first there has been what appears to be a reinforcement of the natural contours of the gritstone outcrop with additional, mainly large stones, complementing natural, in situ boulders. Secondly, there is a magnificent dry-stone rampart to the west. Thirdly, there is a narrow artificial entrance close to the southern end of the rampart. There have even been suggestions that there is a fourth feature - a second, smaller entrance on the eastern side, although this is not at all authenticated.

These carefully placed stones are still clearly visible to observant visitors today although in some locations they have fallen down onto the natural rocks below. Whether that occurred through natural causes over the centuries, or was the result of human interference, for example decommissioning by the invading Roman army or the more peaceful activity of stone-robbing masons building local buildings and walls, remains a matter for conjecture.

In some areas, for example along the southern edge overlooking the main Sheffield to Hathersage road, the 'fortifications' seem to have never been anything more than a simple row of single large boulders or orthostats. In other places they are more carefully placed, similar to dry stone walling.

Some of the natural rock faces, especially to the north and east, today merely challenging to climbers, must have presented a formidable obstacle to anyone contemplating an attack on Carl Wark. One can imagine fierce defenders firing arrows and hurling stones and spears down onto their enemies' heads from these lofty vantage points. But as the majority of the artificial stone defences are not very high, it is possible that timber walls may also have been utilised at some time in the fortifications. There is a wealth of evidence of timber usage in other hillforts and although there is no direct evidence for it at Carl Wark, there are several positions at frequent intervals along the southern wall where wooden posts could possibly have been inserted between the stonework, to support a substantial palisade.

The piece de resistance: the dry-stone, western rampart

The second and most obvious characteristic of Carl Wark is its massive dry-stone wall and rampart. This feature strengthens the weakest natural defence at the western end of the outcrop, where the land descends gradually to a broad, often wet valley. This stone wall is about forty metres long by three metres high, backed on the inside by a rampart some eight metres across its base, tapering inwards to ground level. Its construction is obviously more sophisticated than any of the other stonework around the edges of the promontory. As it stands today the wall averages eight courses of stone, the largest of which is some 1.5 metres long by 0.6 metre wide.

The archaeologist F. G. Simpson cut a trench through this rampart in 1950 during the only known excavation carried out at this site. There is no doubt that after the outcrop itself, the rampart is easily the most noticeable feature of the monument, being easily visible from the top of Higger Tor, from Millstone Edge some distance away and even from Mam Tor. This may have more than a defensive significance: what if the wall had been whitewashed for example, to enhance its visibility for some purpose we don't yet know, or had been built sufficiently high to prevent the curious local population witnessing the secret rituals which took place at its centre?

The narrow entrance

The third main feature of Carl Wark is the narrow, easily defended inturned entrance, situated to the South West corner. It is very close to and clearly linked to the previously described dry-stone rampart. The entrance is about two and a half metres wide by seven metres long, and almost two metres high, although originally the stonework would probably have been still higher resembling the barbican of

CARLWARK RAMPART SECTION. 1950.
(AFTER F.G. SIMPSON)

Reproduced from 'Antiquity' by permission

middle-ages castles, enabling defenders to drop missiles on anyone trying to force an entry. On the surface its form of construction is similar to that of the southern rampart - consisting of rather roughly placed stones which tends to indicate that that the entrance was built at the same time.

The entrance was constructed by skilfully using a combination of natural bedrock, course dry-stone walling and turf, or earth infill. This created a narrow passageway into the hillfort which seems to have been cleverly angled so that any assailants would have to approach with their right, unshielded sides, exposed to any rock-throwing defenders above them. If an assailant did manage to survive the first line of defence there was yet another obstacle to his entry. Close study of the existing and fallen stonework indicates that, as two substantial natural boulders prevent entry either to the left or directly forward, the original direction of entry would most likely have been by turning sharply to the right, again exposing an attacker's weakest side to the defenders.

Yet the dry-stone walling immediately to the right of the entrance appears to be turf or earth backed, so that the original edge of the natural tor may be some four to five metres behind it, the turf serving to fill this area. Excavation would be necessary to prove or disprove whether this is backfilling and whether or not it was contemporaneous with the western rampart. This kind of dating, known by archaeologists as 'terminus post quem', would be achieved if some diagnostic artefact or charcoal which could be subject to dating processes were discovered in the stratigraphy, or layers of material, lying directly below the stonework.

A popular image of hillforts is that they would have possessed substantial wooden gates. At the sight of an approaching enemy the local populace would desperately seek refuge inside with their

SKETCH PLAN OF CARLWARK FORT, HATHERSAGE, DERBYSHIRE.

Reproduced from 'Antiquity' by permission

precious livestock and at the last possible moment the brave defenders would close and barricade the gates. Why is it then that at Carl Wark there is no visible evidence that the entrance ever had any gates? Well, of course, the answer might be that Carl Wark never was a fortress in the first place so gates were never needed. But if at one time it was a fortress, how could its entrance have possibly been defended against attackers without any gates?

Remarkably, the absence of wooden gates may not have been unusual for an Iron Age fort. Some hillforts' occupants are known to have simply relied on felled tree trunks to block their entrances. These could be easily rolled into place in the unlikely event of an emergency. Other defenders were known to have used dense bundles of thorn bushes to protect the hillfort's entrance when they were attacked. Precisely this type of simple but reasonably effective defence was described by Julius Caesar after his army had attacked a hillfort at Bigbury, in 54 BC.

The reason for the occupants favouring these extraordinary methods rather than gates is probably that of technological simplicity - throwing or levering a few prepared tree trunks or bundles of thorns into the entrance is obviously much easier to achieve than the construction and maintenance of gates which would function properly in day to day use, yet be sufficiently strong to resist an attack. Of course the usage of what amount to 'one off' defensive mechanisms like logs or thorns could equally be testimony to the extreme rarity of an attack.

If there had indeed been wooden gates at Carl Wark, it is unlikely that excavation of the entrance could be expected to discover much of their remains. Unfortunately for archaeologists organic material like wood does not usually survive being buried underground for long unless there are special conditions, such as water-logging or permanent freezing, neither of which would apply at Carl Wark, where the soil is highly acidic and only burnt wood would have any chance of survival.

The possibility of there being more than one entrance to Carl Wark has already been briefly mentioned. There is a gap almost in the centre of the steep eastern side which was first referred to in 1911 by Edward Trustram in the Journal of the Derbyshire Archaeological Society. Like other early writers Trustram refers to the monument as Carl's Wark - an apparently earlier variant on the monument's name which was replaced some time later (possibly by the Ordnance Survey) by Carl Wark.

He referred to this entrance as a 'postern gate' and the main purpose of his article was to draw attention to his belief that such entrances were a previously unnoticed feature common to three Derbyshire hillforts. Trustram's postern gate theory was later supported by an amateur archaeologist during a visit in 1913 by the Sheffield-based (and still active) Hunter Archaeological Society. This 'entrance' has been clearly shown on some published plans of Carl Wark (e.g. Bramwell, 1973) but understandably not on others. In particular, it does not appear on the very detailed and authoritative survey published by Piggott in 1948.

Access to it would have been extremely difficult, although it may be relevant that it provides the quickest route to and from the water supply at Burbage Brook and an escape if the main entrance was under threat of being stormed. Whilst today's visitors have created a path through it, its authenticity as a feature of the monument must be considered very doubtful, at least without any further archaeological investigation.

The mystery of Caer's Chair

A large and impressive boulder overhangs the sheer rock face to the north of Carl Wark, tempting the adventurous visitor with a good head for heights to climb out onto its perilous extremity. The stone contains a large hollow which is often half full of water. Was this hollow scooped out by natural erosion or by human endeavour? If natural erosion is the cause then today's deep hollow may have been insignificant at the time Carl Wark was in use. But if it had been carved out then, what purpose might it have served? Perhaps it could have provided the people of Carl Wark with an emergency water supply, or it could have had some ritual significance, much like the font in a church. What should be borne in mind whenever water usage is being considered is that, like many people who live in third world countries today where water is an extremely scarce commodity, their need for it would be extremely small compared to the amount consumed by the average twentieth century household in Britain, with flushing toilets, baths, showers, clothes and dishwashers! Drinking and cooking would be all that Carl Wark's inhabitants would need water for.

The only known artificial hollows were carved out by nineteenth century stonemasons on Stanage to collect water for grouse, but these carvings are quite distinct, so the most likely explanation has to be that the hollow in Caer's Chair is a natural feature.

This curious boulder first appears to have been described by Major Hayman Rooke, an English gentleman and soldier of fortune who visited Carl Wark in the eighteenth century. He recorded his exploits and drew sketches in notebooks. Like other early antiquarians Hayman Rooke imagined that Carl Wark had been built by the Druids. He called the conspicuous boulder 'Car's' or 'Charles's' chair and believed it to have 'been a seat of justice, where the principal Druid

Caer's Chair

sat, who being contiguous to the rock bason (sic) might have recourse to appearances in the water, in doubtful cases. It is natural therefore', he continues enthusiastically, 'to imagine, from the many sacred erections, that this place must have been intended for holy uses, or a court of justice'.

Since Rooke's visit, descriptions of the boulder as 'Caer's Chair' can be found repeated elsewhere, for example in the Sheffield-based and highly respected Clarion Ramblers' records. The boulder has also been referred to as 'Cair's Chair', by another writer who refers to the hillfort as 'Caerl Wark'. He goes on to profess that it is 'a self explanatory name given by a later generation to the handiwork of men of an earlier race'. Yet another writer's explanation is that it is called 'Caelswark' because it is 'a place known even now by its old Saxon name.... i.e. to the work of the Caels, or Gaels - the earliest inhabitants of the islands'. As Caer is generally accepted as Celtic for a fortified place, the two names Caer and Charles seem to have become combined.

Sidney Addy, in his book 'The Hall of Waltheof' of 1893, links the names Carl and Charles to the Norse for Odin. Karl is a Norse name for the 'Old Man' (i.e. the God Odin) and Wark simply means 'fort'. He supports his theory by referring to Charles or Churl Clough on Hallam Moor, near Sheffield and to the Odin Mine at Castleton. Carl's Wark is therefore 'the Old Man's fort'. The Norse for fear or terror is 'yggr' - from which Addy suggests Higger Tor got its name.

What sense can we make today then, out of these mysterious suggestions from so long ago? We are left with a puzzling mixture of names for Carl Wark and its principle natural feature, the curiously shaped boulder, but no proper explanations, even though they may have once seemed self explanatory to some!

Major Hayman Rooke's sketch of Caer's Chair, 1783

Transcript of writing below sketch: 'The view of a remarkable stone called Cars or Charles's Chair; it stands at y^e S.E. end* of a British Work on Hathersage Moor called Charles's Work, on ye top is a large rock bason and near it on ye S. side is a place cut in ye stone big enough for a man to stand upon, from whence it is called Charles's Chair.' This drawing taken Aug: 83.

* Caer's Chair is actually situated on the north side, and shown as such on Rooke's map.

All is not lost, however. It seems logical to suppose that when the intrepid Major Rooke explored the area we now know as the Peak District in the eighteenth century he would have relied totally on knowledgeable local people to guide him to the various places of interest. These congenial members of the community would have related what they knew about the history of each place to him. Their stories may have been embellished by myth and legend, but what is certain is that they would have been completely uninfluenced by outside corruption, due to the lack of any modern methods of communication and media such as television, radio or even books! In fact they may have never had any reason to leave the immediate area of Hathersage throughout their entire lives. Very few people indeed travelled any distance in the eighteenth century, it was difficult and dangerous, so that assisting carters with their loads of millstones to places like Bawtry would probably be the only reason anyone might have had for leaving the valley.

So we can reasonably assume that their account of Carl Wark's origins would be one passed down from generation to generation by word of mouth and would undoubtedly be closer to the truth than any later writer could hope to guess at. So on that basis, the local people seemed to have called the mysterious monument 'Charles' Work'.

Now if we examine the language of the Anglo-Saxons, much of which survives in spoken English today, we find that their word for a 'freeman' was 'Ceorl'. This was actually pronounced 'Churl' and even now we often use the term churlish to describe someone who is rough or vulgarly mannered. The names which were furnished to Rooke in the eighteenth century by his local guides, although spelled differently and perhaps even pronounced differently, are almost certainly Anglo-Saxon in origin. Because pronunciation, writing and particularly spelling in the eighteenth century were imprecise arts and the Celtic for fortified site was Caer, it is easy to understand how Rooke uses the names Caerl or Charles's Work (Wark) in his notes and drawings.

Some other interesting features

Close by the south western corner of Carl Wark are the remains of a small dry-stone building, with a trapezium-shaped trough alongside it carved from a single large rock. Although these works look quite ancient and might be thought to be connected with the building of the rampart, they are consistent with similar post-medieval stonemasons' work which abounds in this area. This was probably the masons' tool shed when they were working in the vicinity, mainly of course, manufacturing millstones. The men were probably also responsible for robbing Carl Wark of many of its 'ready made' ancient stones for their own building work, or for sale to farmers and builders. Who knows, their hovel may have served as an indication that they had staked their claim to the valuable stones in much the same way as mineral prospectors habitually do.

Conflict and Construction

Population and prestige: climatic changes take effect

The landscape around the gritstone edges and tors today is mainly covered in peat, but the area would once have had substantial areas of woodland, not as dense as in the river valleys, but nevertheless a significant source of fuel, building material and tools. These areas of woodland were interspersed with open patches of light, fertile soil, ideally suitable for agriculture, or on the higher ground, for summer pasture.

Although Carl Wark can be glorious on a hot summer day and is a favourite place for families to picnic and perhaps to paddle in the brook below, it is worth remembering that Hathersage Moor can be a bleak and extremely inhospitable place. The Pennines are prone to sudden snow storms which in winter quickly block even the modern the roads. Yet like the landscape, the climate has been inexorably changing over time.

The very earliest inhabitants of the region would have begun to move in around 10,000 years ago when the present warm interglacial period began. They were hunter gatherers, wandering from place to place searching for their food. As the ice sheets retreated northwards the climate gradually became milder so that in Neolithic times the winter weather at Carl Wark was probably nowhere near as severe as it can be today. People began to settle and farm the land, embarking on a more sedentary, agricultural way of life. Then about three thousand years ago, around the beginning of the Iron

Age, the weather began to deteriorate and many of the more exposed farms on the eastern moors had to be abandoned in favour of the valleys. Whether the population level dropped or people were simply displaced is not known, but what is certain is that there was sufficient social stress and turmoil to necessitate the fortification of monuments. During the Iron Age these defended hilltops seem to have become symbols of power and prestige, along with the ownership of cattle, so that by the time of the Roman invasion Britain was a place of petty kingdoms and confederations with ruling elites whose authority was demonstrated by the size and complexity of their hilltop domains. As John Barnatt puts it, the hillforts were the 'nuclear deterrents' of their age.

Other, more subtle ways in which the landscape is changed by human activity can be seen all around Carl Wark today. During the past fifteen years or so thick birch woodland has begun to re-establish itself in the area to the immediate south west of the hillfort, probably initiated by the extensive moorland fires in the 1950's and 60's which caused a change in grazing patterns. Sheep were no longer put out to graze the moorland and so instead of being eaten, the young shoots of trees were able to grow to maturity. Soon the prehistoric forest will have reappeared!

Fortress or folly: was Carl Wark really built for defence?

If, while trying to understand the purpose of Carl Wark, we turn away for a moment from the idea that it was simply built for defence in times of social stress, we are free to consider a range of alternative ideas. For example, we can hypothesise that the site was chosen because it served a symbolic function within a particular area or landscape occupied by its community. For we should remember that what today looks like a wilderness, is in reality an area which has been continuously shaped by centuries of human occupation.

The land around Carl Wark is rich in prehistoric, medieval and post-medieval archaeology. There are prehistoric earthworks, burial and field clearance cairns, barrows, field systems, boundaries and ancient trackways, not to mention the evidence of later medieval and post-medieval gritstone workings.

To digress for a moment, the most fascinating and common examples of these hardy medieval and post-medieval stonemasons' work are the hundreds of abandoned millstones and grindstones, in various stages of manufacture, found all over the area. These are supplemented occasionally with unfinished troughs and other ornamental work. There are several examples of unfinished millstones or the remaining host rocks on Carl Wark itself. An interesting diversion when in the area is to pay a visit to an amazing abandoned open air grindstone 'warehouse', containing approximately four hundred flat edged grindstones. This unique sight can be found close to Bole Hill quarry, almost directly below the bend in the Sheffield to Hathersage road, appropriately known as the Surprise View. Although the exact date that these finely crafted stones were abandoned is not known, it is thought to have occurred either in 1901, when the purchase and subsequent use of the quarry by the Derwent Valley Water Board to provide stone for their dams at Derwent and Howden stopped production, or some time after 1910, when the quarry may have resumed making grindstones. There are also several abandoned ornamental troughs and other stone work to be found towards the Fox House end of Burbage Edge.

We have already seen that Carl Wark is most often referred to in archaeological surveys and literature as an Iron Age hillfort, in other words as a fortress. This is a convenient label, at first sight perhaps even a better term than the somewhat discredited 'hillfort', but it is one which does not even begin to tell us the whole story.

Nevertheless it remains a good starting point for our journey backwards and forwards through time.

For the moment let us suppose that Carl Wark was indeed a fortress. To test the theory that it may have also been an Iron Age fortress we must first consider what period of time constituted the Iron Age and what sort of structure we would expect to find in order to positively define Carl Wark as an Iron Age fortress.

The Iron Age was the last period in the easily understood 'three age' model of prehistory, which was devised in 1819 by a Danish archaeologist called Christian Thomsen, the curator of the National Danish Museum of Antiquities in Copenhagen. It was officially adopted by the British Museum in 1866. Thomsen decided there were two distinct periods before the Iron Age which could for convenience be called the Stone Age and the Bronze Age. Thomsen was arguably the world's first ethno-archaeologist, that is someone who studies modern people's use of stone tools and other artefacts to explain the way in which prehistoric tools might have been used. Today it is widely accepted that his simplistic approach is no longer wholly valid, as there is substantial evidence to show that bronze and perhaps surprisingly, flint implements were still being used well into the Iron Age. Materials such as flint were highly efficient and durable and in prehistoric terms much less costly to produce than iron tools, for example. Indeed, for a long period of time iron artefacts may have had more value as so-called prestige goods than for any functional purposes. For example until methods of hardening and tempering the cutting edges of iron weapons and tools were devised, a flint edge would always outperform metal. Nevertheless, Thomsen's ideas remain very helpful in assisting us to understand the chronology of the past.

View of Carl Wark from the south

*Looking south-east from Higger Tor to Carl Wark
Western rampart clearly visible*

a

*Looking south-west from the interior, showing stone
reinforcement and trackway to Winyard's Nick*

Abandoned millstones, south-west of Carl Wark

b

The dry-stone construction of the western rampart

Looking north along the turf backing of the rampart

c

The entrance, showing left hand side wall

The entrance, viewed from the turf rampart

d

Post-medieval carved gritstone trough and remains of building behind close by south-west corner of Carl Wark

View of interior looking east. There are two possible building platforms at the lower centre and middle right of the photo

View of the interior of Carl Wark looking East

Nearby cairn revealed after moorland fire

f

When exactly was the Iron Age?

As far as we are concerned in Britain the Iron Age dates from approximately 800 BC until AD 43, the time of the Roman army conquest. Change from one 'Age' to another would not have been immediate or even noticeable, of course, so that despite the unquestionable Roman influence, many people living in upland areas would have continued their Iron Age lifestyles well into the first millennium AD.

The Iron Age has been described by one archaeologist as a time 'about which we know so much and yet so tantalisingly little.' It has intrigued some individuals so much that they have gone so far as to recreate Iron Age lifestyles in living experiments. Probably the best and most enduring example is at Butser Iron Age Farm in Hampshire, a unique enterprise which was founded in 1972 by Peter Reynolds. Visitors to Butser can see all aspects of Iron Age living being explored, including the exclusive use of the kinds of tools and implements which would have been available at the time.

However, what is singularly important when considering the origins of Carl Wark is the inescapable fact that the Iron Age was a period especially characterised by the building of an abundance of hillforts. So far so good, but unfortunately all is not as straightforward as it might seem. Whilst the Iron Age is irrevocably connected with the development of defensive hillforts, it is nowhere near certain that Carl Wark was built purely for defensive purposes. Nor for that matter, is it certain that all those hillforts indisputably dated to the Iron Age were actually constructed for defence, rather than for reasons of tribal prestige. This uncertainty surrounding the origins of these types of ancient monuments, shared by the most experienced archaeologists, highlights the difficulties involved in defining their purpose and in ascribing accurate dates to their construction. It is fair to say that there is now no widely accepted definition of a hillfort amongst archaeologists, even though many of these monuments were quite clearly fortresses, intended for defending people and their precious livestock. That alone is clearly insufficient reason to classify every hilltop site as a hillfort. To do so would be to quite wrongly impose unity on a group of enclosures which may actually have had widely different functions, symbolisms and histories.

Many sites like Mam Tor, overlooking today's picture postcard Norman town of Castleton, have clearly been shown to have a history of occupation extending back into the Bronze and Mesolithic ages. Their fortifications may well have resulted from a need to defend what were already immensely long established areas of human activity, which ranged from the earliest nomadic existence of the hunter-gatherers to the later formation of settlements brought about by the development of agricultural way of life.

But again, things are not that simple: for some archaeologists believe that they were in continuous use because of their socio-religious associations rather than out of a need for defence. In other words they had a ritual rather than a military purpose.

Carl Wark is no exception to the doubts which exist about these so called hillforts: even the compilers of the country's most authoritative source, the National Monuments Record, remain safely equivocal on the topic. At one point the official records describe Carl Wark as 'Iron Age' but elsewhere suggest that it may belong to the later Dark Ages - the period of great turmoil after the Romans abandoned Britain - so reflecting the doubts already mentioned.

If we accept for the moment that Carl Wark did indeed serve a defensive or military function during the Iron Age, then it could have stood in isolation, but much more likely is the idea that it would have belonged to what have been termed the 'South Pennine' group of hillforts, which will be discussed later.

Metalworking: an essential skill for the Iron Age

As far as is known no metal artefacts have ever been found on Carl Wark. At first this might be thought to immediately rule out any Iron Age connection, but as is often the case in archaeology things are not that simple. Even where a monument's Iron Age origin is beyond doubt it is not unusual for metal finds from the period to be quite rare. This is due to the natural corrosion of the metal and the decomposition of associated wooden objects over the centuries. A golden rule in archaeology is that absence of evidence should never be taken as evidence of absence!

So whether or not iron (or bronze for that matter) was ever smelted at or close by Carl Wark remains a mystery. If it was, where would the raw materials for any iron smelting have come from? One theory is that the metal could have been crudely obtained by melting the relatively small iron nodules to be found in the millstone grit, but this seems very unlikely. The most likely explanation is that iron would have been traded from other people who came from areas where ironstone was mined. Another possibility which has only recently begun to be considered is that Iron Age people used bog iron as their source of raw material. Ochre coloured streaks are often seen in moorland bogs and very recently archaeologists in the Peak District have discovered evidence to suggest that iron may have somehow been extracted from them, but more investigation is needed in this area before that source can be confirmed.

Where are the ghosts?

Was Carl Wark ever inhabited? Did people actually live and die here or did Carl Wark serve some other purpose? At first glance the interior of the enclosure appears unable to have sufficient space for the construction of any substantial buildings. Its surface is very uneven and crowded with huge, immovable boulders. Visitors familiar with other hillforts or hill top settlements will immediately realise that there are no remains of hut platforms to be seen on Carl Wark, unlike for example, the summit of Mam Tor, where there are dozens cut into the hillside, still clearly visible even today. Despite this apparent lack of evidence, it needs to be understood that even if Carl Wark had been occupied, there need not necessarily have been many houses there at all. Archaeologists have already discovered that whereas some hillforts had hundreds of houses, others only had one or two. Whilst the reasons for this may not be clear the numerical findings are indisputable.

Of course, like any other 'settlement', ancient or modern, not all the buildings in a hilltop enclosure would have been houses and constant rebuilding would take place. Some structures would have been mainly used for the safe storage of food, both against the elements and as emergency supplies in a crisis. Others might have been workshops, still more used to house animals.

In trying to establish whether the interior of Carl Wark could have been occupied, it is worth comparing the relative sizes of known buildings discovered during excavations elsewhere. Two good examples are at Danebury, in Hampshire and at Breiddin, in Powys where lengthy excavations have revealed a great deal about life in an Iron Age hilltop enclosure. In fact Danebury is probably the most intensively studied hillfort in Britain, having been excavated and reported upon for many years by a team led by Professor Barry

Cunliffe. Danebury dates from the 6th century BC, when the defences consisted of a single bank and ditch, with two entrances. The interior contained quarries, storage pits, rectangular four-poster granaries and roundhouses - ranging from five to seven metres in diameter - arranged along 'metalled' streets.

Danebury was densely populated, with its busy inhabitants crowded together in circular houses set around the inner edge of the ramparts. Occupation was continuous, intensive and controlled, perhaps by a ruling elite. Like many other hillforts, Danebury was re-fortified around 400 BC when a second rampart was erected and modifications made to the eastern entrance to create an easily defended, curved entrance passage. It is thought to have become uninhabited during the 1st century, perhaps only being used after then as a refuge.

The Breiddin hillfort, in Powys, lies in the northern half of a dense band of large and medium sized hillforts which extend along the Wye valley and the tributaries of the Severn into the Welsh Marches and on towards North Wales. Excavations led by Chris Musson have showed that after sporadic activity in the Mesolithic and late Neolithic/early Bronze Ages, substantial occupation occurred towards the end of the Bronze Age. A timber framed rampart yielded radiocarbon dates centred on 800 BC. At about the 3rd century BC it was rebuilt and strengthened. A third rampart was probably added later. There is no evidence that occupation extended beyond the 1st century AD and early Roman material was absent. Occupation began again in the 2nd or early 3rd century AD and continued until the end of the Roman period. An important collection of waterlogged wooden objects from about 300 BC was recovered from Buckbean pond, within the hillfort.

Of particular interest is the discovery of evidence for numerous circular and rectangular buildings inside the hillfort. Musson's team has categorised them into three generic types of buildings: roundhouses, four-posters and six-posters.

Roundhouses, which are the structures believed to most likely to have been used mainly as dwellings, ranged from five metres to seven metres in diameter and Breiddin was fairly densely occupied over much of what Musson calls its 'buildable' area. This finding may well be highly relevant to a small settlement such as Carl Wark.

This type of comparison helps us to establish the possible sizes of buildings which could have been built on Carl Wark, if it were indeed occupied. The question is what form would they have taken? Would they have been similar to those at Breiddin, perhaps sharing function if not form, or might they have been more local in their characteristics? Bronze Age houses in the Peak District were circular, with wooden poles supporting a turf roof, although a very small number (an example being at Swine Sty near Baslow) had low drystone walls. But the overwhelming majority would have been timber buildings, consisting of wooden poles inserted into post-holes in the ground, supporting wattle and daub walls.

At Breiddin, some structures had roofs reaching to the ground, like wigwams, but with their entrances flanked by stout posts. Occasionally a level platform would be cut into sloping ground to accommodate the building. Four and six-poster buildings were of various sizes, averaging 2.5 metres between posts. These buildings were probably stores or specialised agricultural buildings, although again, some may have been dwellings. Delicate excavation would be necessary to reveal evidence of post holes from houses of this type at Carl Wark as very often only a subtle change in soil colouring indicates their presence.

Reconstructed Iron Age Roundhouse at Butser

Of further significance in the investigation of any possible occupancy of Carl Wark, is a feature common to other hillforts like Danebury and Breiddin. Their buildings were situated closely adjacent to their ramparts, as if their occupants felt more secure nestled up against the walls. Given the known sizes of those buildings, this information is useful for assessing which areas of Carl Wark might have been utilised as building areas. Such an area is apparent for a considerable length alongside the western and southern ramparts. Careful examination of the interior reveals a number of other possible sites, either between the protection of the massive boulders or perhaps utilising them as partial shelters.

The only area which seems to have any visible surface irregularity is near the entrance. Even then these may actually be the results of the limited excavations undertaken in 1950. Very often features not apparent on the ground can be seen from the air, but aerial photographs taken of the site do not reveal any traces of buildings.

As there are no visible signs of occupancy, only further investigation by what are called geophysical methods, such as magnetometry (which measures the electromagnetic properties of buried features and the soil to indicate subsurface anomalies), or ground penetrating radar would test the hypothesis. Of course trial excavations would then be needed to verify the scientific findings.

Making a living: everyday life and trade in the surrounding area

Assuming that people did once live on or certainly around Carl Wark, where did they grow their crops and tend their animals when they were not safely tucked away inside their fort? What evidence is visible on the present landscape to indicate whether in fact anyone might have lived or farmed in the immediate area?

One ancient trackway crosses a small fertile plain, below the southern edge of the hillfort. A group of 15 cairns, a hut and circular hut floor, a hearth, and a flint working floor were all found south west of here in 1926 by W. M. Cole. One cairn contained an urn and a bronze implement, now in Sheffield Museum. A short time spent field walking here, particular in winter when the heather and bracken provides less cover, will be rewarded by the discovery of a Bronze Age stone clearance or field boundary and particularly in the area to the south east, over twenty cairns and barrows can be plainly seen.

Slightly further to the west at a gully called Winyard's Nick, a dark green rubbing stone from Langdale was found. As well as being functional these beautiful artefacts were often regarded as highly prized prestige goods and were widely traded. This find may indicate that this was a trade route from the Lake District although it is more likely that the artefact was simply dropped and lost at some time. Most of the Neolithic axes found in North Derbyshire originate in Cumbria, but others come from as far afield as Leicestershire and Cornwall.

Winyard's Nick, to the west of Carl Wark, is a deep pass worn away by ancient travellers crossing over Millstone Edge. It is clearly visible on the horizon from long distances away, which would eventually have enabled the packhorse drivers, known as 'jaggers' or 'coggers' to aim accurately for the crossing from anywhere on the moor. The remains of a necklace made from jet was found by L. H. Butcher in the same area in 1961. Jet is a shiny black shale, reminiscent of coal. Its production is usually associated with Whitby, on the east coast, but similar jewellery was once hand crafted locally from cannel coal seams. One such Bronze Age 'factory' was discovered on Totley Moor, between Carl Wark and Sheffield, after the disastrous moorland fires of 1959. Worked shale has also been discovered at Birchen Edge, at Barbrook and at Swine Sty, all near Baslow.

To return to Carl Wark itself, the fact that its entrance faces south may indicate a relationship between it and the occupiers of that area as it would appear to be common sense to have the entrance facing their main area of activity and/or communication for ease and rapidity of access, both in everyday use and especially in a crisis if Carl Wark had a defensive purpose. In effect, it was their front door.

What were the main lines of communication in the vicinity which preceded today's congested roads? Carl Wark is situated amongst a network of ancient trackways, the origins of some being uncertain, but which date back to the very earliest days of inter-community trade. A few of these tracks remain rights of way even today, but many are no longer considered such, having been abandoned or cut off by the nineteenth century enclosures. Those that remain are only discernible because travellers, on horse or foot, have eroded deep, often parallel, ruts in the surface of the moorland over centuries of use. Some are known to have been specially constructed as packhorse trails or for carting peat and stone. In places the ruts caused by animals and vehicles became impassable each time there was heavy rain, forcing travellers to take alternative, parallel paths and leading to the formation of what John Barnatt, Senior Survey Archaeologist for the Peak District National Park Authority, has appropriately called 'braided hollow-ways'. Reference to the origins of trackways can sometimes be detected in names such as 'Jaggers Lane' - 'jagger' or 'cogger' being a term used for pack men.

There are visible tracks, not shown on maps, passing from east to west immediately to the north of the hillfort and north to south on the eastern side of Carl Wark, from Sheffield towards Hathersage. A similar track passes immediately to the south of the hillfort coming from the direction of Holmesfield, a settlement with a long history of occupation, south of Sheffield, towards Hathersage. This route was turnpiked in 1781 and although it deviates in places from the original track, is basically the road we see today. Taken as a whole, these tracks, which are typical of those found on the Eastern moors, form a fairly tight network around Carl Wark and, provided at least some of them are contemporary to it, would have provided easy access.

If Carl Wark was intended as one of the previously mentioned South Pennines group of hillforts, it can be said to be strategically placed as far as the river Noe is concerned. Whilst invaders would prefer to use existing trade routes and other ready made tracks than follow marshy, heavily wooded, insect infested river valleys, rivers remained important alternative routes for invaders to utilise as they made their way inland. If a river was navigable boats could be used, but even if it were not, it might be easier to follow the banks of a river than to battle one's way through thick, virgin forest. And of course, so much easier to find one's way back again! This has particular relevance for the proposition, discussed later, that Carl Wark may have been intended to prevent a Saxon incursion. But that is leaping too far ahead in the story.

Searching for the origins of Carl Wark: archaeological finds in the vicinity

Having described Carl Wark and the surrounding area in detail, what sort of evidence is available to explain its origins? How can we begin to understand what its construction means? From the detailed study of other monuments it seems likely that Carl Wark was probably first utilised in an already widely exploited landscape because one, or perhaps both, of two crucial social needs arose. The first was secular: the basic need for defence. The second was probably spiritual: the need to hold ritual gatherings.

What is certain is that people had always been active around the site. Evidence of the earliest human activity in the immediate vicinity of Carl Wark is provided by finds of Mesolithic flint implements and arrow heads all around - at Over Owler Tor, Winyard's Nick, Higger Tor and Burbage Moor. The only artefact known to have actually been found on Carl Wark is a flint blade or 'slug knife', said to be Bronze Age.

As this appears to be a stray find, it cannot provide any absolute or relative date for Carl Wark itself. In fact what this small number of finds proves is very difficult to say. Was the landscape which surrounds Carl Wark occupied more or less continuously since the appearance of the very first humans in the region, or was occupation sporadic - perhaps occurring only for a short time every thousand years?

Carl Wark resurrected: could there have been two phases of construction?

If the construction of Carl Wark can be thought of as being in two distinct phases the possibility of it having originally started life as a symbolic enclosure and then later having been converted into a defended hillfort becomes a serious consideration. For this explanation to be feasible we need to find some evidence that Carl Wark was originally a Neolithic enclosure used for ritual gatherings.

The line of rocks used to 'defend' the southern side may in fact have served to delineate the boundaries, both physical and spiritual, of the ritual activities which took place on Carl Wark. Today at least they look more suitable for that purpose than for resisting a determined attack. Helpful comparisons can be made between what can be seen at Carl Wark and the recently excavated stone enclosure at Gardom's Edge, about seven kilometres to the south, near Baslow. This enclosure was once thought to be a hillfort but has now, after several year's of investigation by the Peak National Park Authority and the University of Sheffield's archaeologists, been convincingly shown to be a Neolithic ceremonial enclosure. Just like at Carl Wark, the builders of Gardom's Edge used an almost straight natural gritstone edge as part of its boundary. As Gardom's Edge is not an outcrop but an escarpment, the builders completed their enclosure with a curved linear stone embankment connecting two points on the edge about five hundred metres apart.

Evidence for associated ritual activity at Gardom's Edge is provided by a rare example of a magnificent Bronze Age cup and ring marked stone which lies outside, but close to the enclosure. This example is one of the largest and best preserved, although in the summer of 1995 extraordinary steps were taken by archaeologists to preserve the weather eroded and vandalised stone for posterity by producing a latex mould from which a durable and exact polyester replica was manufactured. The replica was airlifted onto the moors to replace the original stone which was carefully buried, so as to be available for study in the future when scientific techniques will have improved considerably. A similar replica is on display in Sheffield Museum. Underlining the ritual importance of this site is the presence nearby of a monolith, or upright standing stone. Again, this is outside the enclosure, but is close enough to be associated with both it and the cup and ring marked stone. These rare stones are believed to have had important ritual significance but exactly what the intricately carved patterns means remains a mystery. Some archaeologists associated the discovery of cup marks, or individual small carved cups and upright standing stones with fertility rites.

Unfortunately, there do not seem to be any similar features to these associated with Carl Wark. Nevertheless, an important piece of evidence is that this type of enclosure obviously does not present a formidable obstacle to an enemy. The stones at Gardom's Edge and most of Carl Wark do not seem to have been part of a substantial defensive wall, as many are odd shapes and stand upright, rather than being laid down flat in the fashion of a dry stone wall. Their function is symbolic rather than practical. In fact, if the massive western rampart is ignored for the moment, Carl Wark looks even less like a defended enclosure than some parts of Gardom's Edge. To have been effective in defending its occupants it would need at the very least to have been enhanced with something like a substantial timber framework.

Two scenarios may have followed Carl Wark's use in Neolithic times as a centre for ritual activities. Either the enclosure was no longer needed for ritual purposes and was abandoned; or deep social stress and the threat of conflict forced the society which utilised Carl Wark to modify it for their defence. In other words what was once a church became a castle.

This second phase would have been marked by the building of the western rampart and its associated entrance: what we can consider to be the first real fortifications. But here lies a problem: this account does not explain the enormous contrast between the effectiveness of the dry stone rampart and the ineffectiveness of the earlier, simple stone enclosure, which was not strengthened in the same way. Of course one possibility is that for some reason the work was abandoned before any further upgrading of the defences could be achieved. Perhaps the inhabitants surrendered, or were defeated in a short, fierce battle with an enemy. More mundanely, the stones may have simply been carted off during later millennia by stonemasons and farmers.

Even if Carl Wark was not built in two phases but in one, the same difficulty arises and the conclusion has to be that it was either left relatively low and unfinished, or as previously mentioned, the stonework was backed by timber which has long ago disappeared. If there had been any wood involved, it has rotted away. There is no visible evidence of Carl Wark's timber defences being burnt - where this has occurred elsewhere it has generated such fierce heat that the surrounding rocks melted.

Unique features: the western rampart and entrance

The most intact and impressive feature of Carl Wark is its western rampart and the nearby entrance, which dominate the monument.

Both consist of well made dry-stone walling backed by turf or soil. But when and why were these features constructed? Can they really be said to be a 'second phase' of construction, or are they contemporaneous with the other defensive stonework? We have already seen that the limited excavation carried out at Carl Wark failed to provide an answer. How then, might the date of their construction be ascertained?

The dating of individual objects and the chronology of a monument's construction can be ascertained by a number of methods. The most fundamental method used by archaeologists during excavations is stratification, which is based on the principle that if one layer of material is found lying on top of another, the lower layer must have been deposited earlier in time.

Probably the most important advance ever made in the techniques available for ascertaining the age of certain objects is radio carbon dating, which is based on the fact that when a living organism dies, carbon-14 atoms in the organism begin to decay at a measurable rate.

Wooden items can often be dated by dendrochronology - the comparison of tree rings, and in fact carbon 14 dating has been made more accurate through comparison with ancient wooden objects whose age was exactly known. Other scientific methods are available for dating pottery, hearths, ovens, kilns and so on, whilst on a more empirical level, comparison with similar types or designs of artefact and monuments remains an important method and at the moment the only one available as far as Carl Wark is concerned.

When Carl Wark was excavated in 1950, the archaeologists were unable to find any evidence in the stratification from which they could date the rampart. This was of course before the development of carbon-14 dating so they may have actually discovered carbon deposits which would be invaluable today but they would simply not have had any reason then to preserve them. That being the case, it is necessary to investigate other sources of information for the possible date of construction by comparing the development of hillforts and in particular, Carl Wark's main features, with those found elsewhere in Britain.

There is plenty of evidence that a massive re-fortification of some hillforts occurred in Britain around 400 BC, particularly in the southern parts of Britain. This may have been a national response to some as yet unidentified threat or perhaps a phenomenon confined to the south which only occasionally occurred elsewhere. This threat could have been external, in other words from invaders, or internal, perhaps from intertribal struggles or even disease, such as smallpox. In many places extra ramparts and ditches were added to already defended enclosures. But the most interesting development at this time of crisis was that the entrances to hillforts were made much more complex.

The straightforward simplicity of Carl Wark's entrance does not seem to indicate a similar development, but both the rampart and entrance, if they were a second phase in the construction, most certainly constitute a major re-fortification of what had originally existed. But dating Carl Wark on evidence based on the entrance type is nowhere near conclusive. Despite their inhabitants constructing wonderfully complex modifications at some sites, a survey of 900 univallate (i.e. single walled) hillforts by Forde-Johnston showed that 85 to 90% only ever have had simple 'gap type' entrances, just like Carl Wark.

An alternative explanation for the sudden appearance of these complex preparations for warfare could be that they were prestige developments. They were intended to impress visitors from other societies or tribes, for all the same reasons that town councils today indulge in expensive pomp and ceremony or lavish vast amounts of their scarce financial resources on questionable projects by which they might be remembered long after their demise!

After this period of activity and apparent alarm, there is some evidence to suggest that Britain may have entered a period of relative calm. This lead to the uncomfortable hillforts being abandoned in favour of a more pleasant life in open villages. These villages would be scattered peacefully amongst the hillforts and probably quickly replaced them as the focus of community activity. Bredon Hill, in Hereford and Worcester is thought to be such an example. Here an extensive village, with houses and non-defensive enclosures, dating from 250-50 BC and covering several hectares has been discovered. So the once thriving hillforts may have become deserted, exposed hilltops, rarely visited by anyone except the most energetic with time on their hands to explore what would, within a couple of short generations, become dusty relics of the past.

The next direct threat would have arisen as a result of the vast upheaval caused by the terrifying invasion by the Romans in 43 AD. Even the inhabitants of colossal hillforts such as Maiden Castle, in Dorset, were forced to make last minute, panic stricken modifications to their fortifications. These must have been desperate times, but the native population's attempts to repel the disciplined might of the Roman Army were futile. The Roman military machine had already gained vast experience throughout Europe of laying siege to and destroying the best defences. Their strategy was simple: they would slaughter a percentage of the occupants mercilessly and then take the men, women and children that they spared into slavery. Unsurprisingly, some defenders simply abandoned their hilltop refuges, apparently recognising the superiority of the invaders and surrendering to them without resistance, rather than risking an inevitable and bloody defeat.

It seems reasonable to assume that by the time the Roman army reached the upland areas of the Peak District, preparations for fight or flight had irrevocably been decided upon by the indigenous population's leaders. For example a number of old Iron Age hillforts are known to have been reoccupied in Scotland and Wales immediately prior to the arrival of Agricola. Who were these occupants likely to have been?

The Celtic Tribes of Britain

Turbulent Times: the Roman invasion and its aftermath

By the time of the Roman invasion, society in Britain had become divided into many distinct tribes, each controlling their own territories. The area around Carl Wark at the time of the Roman invasion came under the jurisdiction of the largest Celtic, or British tribe. They were called the Brigantes, a name which means 'upland people' and they occupied the greater part of northern Britain. Their boundaries stretched from the Cheviots to somewhere south of the present day Derbyshire border, where a tribe known as the Coritani held possession. Less sophisticated than their eastern neighbours, the Parisi, the Brigantes were described by Caesar as people who 'for the most part do not grow corn but live on milk and meat and dress in skins'. Areas of population would be separated by wild moorland and thick forests, so that political cohesion would have been slower to emerge amongst the Brigantes than some other tribes, although by the time Claudius invaded Britain in AD 43 some stability had probably been achieved.

These tribal structures were unsophisticated and lacked any properly developed political system. Nor, broadly speaking, did they boast any elite groups which might have been capable of motivating people sufficiently to organise the development of large scale fortifications. There were notable exceptions to this though, at places like Stanwick, in North Yorkshire and Almondbury, in West Yorkshire.

Despite this, the Brigantes seemed to have had a recognisable network of about twenty hillforts in the South Pennines, of which, as previously mentioned, Carl Wark may well have been one. This group includes Mam Tor, Fin Cop, Almondbury, Wincobank, Shirecliffe, Burr Tor, Brierly Common, Markland Grips, Coombs Moss, Whinny Hill and Gilbert Hill. With one exception they are related to rivers which ultimately flow to the east coast.

In addition to their forts, they built other major defensive structures. The linear earthwork today known as the 'Roman Rig', which runs all the way from Wincobank, in Sheffield, to the River Dearne valley in the east, may have been a Brigantian work, intended to resist the Roman threat, rather than being a post-Roman development. Pottery known as Brigantian ware, first discovered and subsequently named by Sir Mortimer Wheeler at Stanwick, has been found at Wincobank, in Sheffield and at Mam Tor. Carl Wark lies almost directly between the two.

So it is distinctly possible that Carl Wark, together with the network of forts to which it may have belonged, formed an integral part of the Brigantian's border defences against the threat posed by their restless neighbours the Coritani, living to the south.

Another alternative is that the building of the rampart and entrance may have been the Brigantian's response to another, even greater threat, that of the new invaders. The Roman army is believed to have first attacked the Brigantes some time around AD 71 - AD 74. What must it have been like to face these adversaries from the mighty Roman Empire? Would the stone rampart have done its job?

The Roman army was well-versed in quickly gaining military control of an area: if the local populace was friendly all well and good, if not hostages would be taken to ensure their future good behaviour. Then a fort would be built. Navio was the closest Roman fort to Carl

Wark, built by Flavian's battle-hardened soldiers out of earth and timber and occupied from about AD 75 - 150. Its purpose was to oversee North Derbyshire and ensure the continued subjugation of the local population.

The building of Navio raises an interesting question: Carl Wark may have been abandoned centuries earlier, but if it was still in use when Navio was built, its proximity to the Roman military presence makes it difficult to understand why it was not attacked and destroyed, something which, not surprisingly, occurred at some other hillforts. The Wrekin, in Shropshire, was sacked by the Roman army around AD 48-50, whilst Cadbury Castle, in Somerset was defeated in AD 60. And there are other examples of the Roman army displaying its superiority.

Yet despite this, as the Roman remains in the South Pennines seem to be predominantly military in nature, with very few exceptions such as a villa at Carsington, the indications are that the region's population must have continued to be restless, stubbornly resisting all the Empire's efforts to subjugate them. But the stone faced rampart, if it was built at this turbulent time, mysteriously remains relatively intact, despite Carl Wark's proximity to the Roman forts and their network of roads.

If we assume for a moment that Carl Wark was in use and was strengthened by the local population during the Roman invasion we can consider a number of alternative scenarios. One explanation could be that the stone rampart was built to resist the impending Roman invasion, but the Brigantes abandoned it during the early years of Roman occupation when their queen, Cartimandua, capitulated. A second possibility is that Carl Wark was fortified by the followers of Cartimandua's estranged husband, Venutius, who led a Brigantian revolt in AD 69.

Unfortunately these explanations are based on the assumption that the Brigantes were well organised, whereas the most likely scenario for Iron Age military activity in Britain may well have been very different - certainly nowhere approaching that of the Roman Army. Instead of leaders and their armies combining forces Iron Age warfare was probably based on notions of individual prestige gained through minor skirmishes and raiding other settlements for cattle.

Of course there remains the possibility that Carl Wark was a post-Roman era development, a defensive structure built after the Roman soldiers had left the area for good. Critically, the design of the stone and turf rampart, which has already been described in detail, may provide the key to this particular question. According to the archaeologist C. M. Piggott, the rampart is unlike any other fortification in the north of England, an opinion which led him to believe it necessary to look for evidence of the introduction of this particular method of construction in other parts of Britain. One thing is worth noting: the Roman Army had always favoured the use of turf in its fortifications, probably because the natural material was readily available, easily cut and easily handled. They utilised turf in the construction of the permanent Hadrian and Antonine walls, which separated Scotland from England and in their own temporary marching camps.

Most large Roman towns, or civitas-capitals as they were known, received earthwork defences in the late second or early third century, in a process which took some fifty years to complete. An example of improved urban defences utilising stone walls and earth banks can be seen in the sequence of defensive works at Lincoln, where a wall similar in style to that found at Carl Wark, although admittedly far more sophisticated, was constructed.

What is important to note is that this improvement did not occur until the second and third centuries AD. It is also reasonable to assume that this sort of improvement would only be carried out at first at most important or vulnerable locations, before it became common elsewhere in the country. London's walls were built some time after ca AD 190, confirmed by the finding of moulds for counterfeiting silver dinarii along with some genuine coins in a rubbish pit beneath the walls.

There can be no doubt that it would be quite a while before people occupying the remote uplands of the Peak District would become aware of the technique. From this sort of detailed comparison Piggott deduced that the similarity of style of construction used in Carl Wark's rampart to that of the wall at Lincoln, strongly suggests that it would not have been constructed before Romans introduced the technique and very probably not constructed any earlier than the third century AD.

If it was constructed whilst the Roman soldiers were still in occupation nearby, interesting questions are raised. It would clearly have to have been built either with their consent, or more remarkably still, in defiance of their mighty presence. Yet it is inconceivable that such a small, poorly defended hilltop could have withstood even a half-hearted Roman assault, given the ferocity of the army, its military ability and if the worse came to the worse, its habit of laying siege for as long as it took to call up reinforcements or starve out the trapped occupants.

To give an idea of what was available to the Roman commander in case of a local revolt, the Roman forts built in the region between AD 54-70 were typically garrisoned by a cohort of 500 auxiliary troops, whose main duties would have included regularly patrolling the roads and generally enforcing the occupation. The nearest fort, at Navio, was garrisoned by a cohort from Aquitaine.

Templeborough's garrison, to the east of Sheffield, was the base for the Fourth Cohort of Gauls and was a much bigger enterprise, probably totalling 1000 men, including 240 cavalry. These formidable troops were only a day's march away from Carl Wark. Any resistance would have been brief, bloody and utterly futile.

Despite the apparent hopelessness of indulging in resistance, there will always be brave, idealistic individuals prepared to take the risks involved. Opposition to the Roman army did occasionally occur in some places and large areas of Britain were probably never conquered in the true sense of the word, despite the impressive propaganda of contemporary Roman writers, who described a 'well co-ordinated invasion and subjugation', presumably exactly the kind of report their masters in Rome wished to hear!

Flight to fight: the Romans temporarily withdraw from the region

In AD 140 Agricola had to withdraw the Roman army from the Peak District to provide reinforcements to be sent northwards to Scotland where serious frontier incidents had occurred at Hadrian's wall, built in AD 122. As part of that risky withdrawal process Navio, then only a wooden construction but nevertheless substantial, was dismantled to prevent the local people from occupying it. In the rest of the region only Templeborough remained garrisoned. Roman patrols would no longer have passed near Carl Wark from the time of the withdrawal until around AD 158, when Navio was reoccupied and rebuilt, this time in stone, as a direct response to the activities of the Brigantes.

So there is a possibility that Carl Wark's rampart was built during the period of time between AD 140 and AD 158 when the area was free from the occupation of the Roman army. That would explain why its construction reflects to some extent the methods the Romans themselves used, although not necessarily explaining its survival to the present day relatively unscathed. Motivation for the construction could have been an intention to resist their return, although this seems unlikely given the previously mentioned military capability of Rome's armies. If that sort of miscalculation had been made, Carl Wark would have simply been abandoned when the Romans eventually returned from Scotland in AD 158.

Alternatively, Carl Wark could have been built as a means for self-defence in the belief that the Roman army would never again return. In that case the aggressors would be other British tribes or fresh invaders from overseas.

Could Carl Wark have been built with consent of the Roman army?

Another theory already mentioned, which at first sight seems highly improbable, is that the stone rampart was built by the Brigantes during time of the Roman occupation and with the consent of the Roman military commander. Could such a remarkable event have occurred? There is in fact a precedent for this apparently extraordinary idea which occurred in Wales. Around the beginning of the 2nd century some Welsh hillforts appeared which could not have been constructed without the knowledge and the consent of the Roman government. The most likely explanation is that these hillforts were built at the Romans' instigation after enrolling their militia as a kind of irregular native force for the defence of their own country, albeit under Roman rule. But if this had been true for Carl Wark, the hillfort could be expected to show other, easily visible signs of occupation associated with this period, such as stone houses and related buildings, which it simply does not.

As none of the evidence so far discussed can conclusively place the development of the stone rampart in the Roman occupation era, our investigations must focus on what happened at Carl Wark after the Roman army permanently withdrew from the region and left Britain for good.

The end of Roman civilisation: the beginning of the Dark Ages

In a strange paradox it might well have been said by many who had prospered under the Roman occupation that the lights were going out all over Britain when the occupying army finally withdrew. The ensuing period, known as the Dark Ages, was aptly named, not just because of the collapse of a civilisation, but because so very little is known about the period, even today. Quite simply, the authority of the Roman Empire collapsed and with it the necessity or the motivation to record history disappeared.

Yet, after four centuries, the soldiers stationed in this far flung outpost of the Roman Empire would have integrated into the native population. Some, whilst Roman subjects, would have Roman soldiers and British women as parents - a grave marker at Templeborough is evidence of this kind of intermarriage. So, at the end of the Roman occupation, many of the ruling elite were probably culturally more British than Roman. They had never lived anywhere else, probably never visited Rome, and chose to remain in Britain.

When would this momentous event have taken place? Pottery evidence from Navio indicates that the fort was inhabited until the early part of the fourth century, whilst according to the Romans' own records, military activity in the Southern Pennines ceased around AD 360. By AD 411 Rome had officially told Britain that it had to defend itself, formally marking the end of Roman rule in Britain, as the once massive empire slowly imploded.

Whilst the situation immediately following the ending of Roman rule in Britain is still very unclear, it is known that some hillforts, such as the one at South Cadbury, in Somerset for example, were re-fortified for defence against other Celtic tribes. In southern and eastern areas re-fortification was more probably a response to a new threat: Anglo-Saxon incursions, which were already occurring in many areas of Britain.

In an almost post-apocalyptic fashion some important Roman towns such as Silchester (Calleva Altrebatum) in Hampshire, were entirely abandoned, their civilised splendour being allowed to fall into ruin, but occupation continued or was renewed in the majority of cases. Even then many individual buildings were abandoned, whilst the use and quality of pottery declined and gold and silver coinage was buried - the hoarding of coins is always a sign of deep social unrest.

So Carl Wark and other similar sites may have been important elements in the confusion of the fourth to sixth centuries, as the various British tribes jostled for territory and power in the vacuum left by the autocratic Romans, particularly so in the more remote and relatively uncivilised upland regions such as the Peak District.

Describing Carl Wark in his 1948 survey, the archaeologist C. M. Piggott unambiguously takes the view that the stone rampart is a Dark Age construction. It is worth quoting his comment that 'students of Iron Age forts in the highland zone of Britain will immediately be aware that there is nothing familiar in the defensive structure of Carl Wark.' He then draws comparisons with the defences at a Scottish hillfort known as Traprain Law, in Lothian. These observations, coupled with his conviction that the use of turf was a technique introduced by the Roman army and which only became a tradition amongst the British people in later years, leads him to propose a 5th or 6th century date (or even later) for the western rampart, making

Carl Wark quite definitely a 'British' fort, ruling out any possibility of it being Iron Age or even Romano-British, as previously put forward by other commentators.

If Piggott is correct, what was the grave threat which galvanised the builders of Carl Wark into action? What other evidence is there of defensive measures being taken in the region at this time which might support the notion that it belongs to this much later period?

More trouble: the Anglo-Saxon invasion

Whether they had liked them or not, the departure of their Roman 'protectors' left the Celtic, or British population, immediately vulnerable to any new invaders daring and skilled enough to cross the seas which surrounded and isolated the British Isles. Although the people of the Southern Pennines were protected to a great degree by the extensive Humber marshes and thick forests, they would finally need to depend on their network of hillforts if they were to successfully resist being the victims of a barbaric onslaught and avoid being subjugated once more.

As well as their hillforts it is known that other measures were taken to prevent incursions by invaders. One example is an earthwork known as the Grey Ditch, which crosses the Roman Road from Navio to Buxton in Bradwell Dale. This feature may have formed part of the local defences, intended to prevent invaders arriving up the Noe valley and gaining access to the uplands to the south. This earthwork, coupled with the distinct absence of Anglian material any earlier than the sixth century in graves excavated in the area suggests that the Anglo-Saxons eventually reached this region later than elsewhere in Britain. Whether they came as outright invaders or through political intermarriage is not known.

This late arrival could have been due to the natural difficulties caused by the terrain, or alternatively, by their meeting fierce resistance and well placed system of defensive works, which might have included Carl Wark. Alternatively, the Grey Ditch may have been a much later Anglian frontier line as the invaders in turn struggled with the British for control of the region to the north of their kingdom of Mercia.

New Kingdoms: Mercia, Northumbria and the coming of the Danes

The Anglian kingdom of Mercia - the old English name 'Mierce' means 'the borderers' - roughly constituted present day Derbyshire and the Midlands. Although the socio-political situation in the area during the 6th to 9th centuries is poorly understood, it may be that Mercia's northern border with Northumbria once ran close to Carl Wark and 'border skirmishes' between subjects of the rival kingdoms may have been common. There may even have been a separate, 'client' kingdom in the Hope Valley, retaining its autonomy whilst paying appropriate dues to its larger neighbours.

Whatever the situation, as is so often the case in troubled times peace could only be reached through compromise and in AD 829 an historic event took place in the picturesque village of Dore, situated to the west of Sheffield and significantly only five kilometres to the east of Carl Wark. The Anglo Saxon Chronicle records that at Dore, King Eanred of Northumbria surrendered to King Ecgbert of Wessex, who had previously conquered Mercia, so that in effect the country of England as we know it today was created. A shield-shaped plaque mounted on a stone set in Dore village green commemorates the momentous occasion. The inscription on the stone reads, 'King Ecgbert of Wessex led his army to Dore in the year AD 829 against King Eanred of Northumbria by whose submission King Ecgbert became first Overlord of England'. Given the proximity of Dore village could it be that the descendants of the people who built Carl Wark were present to witness the historic surrender at Dore?

Yet despite the treaty the English were not to live in peace for very long. In the late ninth century, it was the turn of the Danish army to repeat the seemingly endless process of invasion and occupation in the region. This new threat raises the distinct possibility that Carl Wark's defences were contemporaneous to these later events. But the Danes were a literate race and much that happened at this time was recorded in their historical documents or charters - for example Dore is mentioned once again, by King Edmund in 942, as being on the boundary of Mercia, whilst a tenth century charter refers to Danes holding land in the Hope Valley - yet there is no known written mention of Carl Wark. Given the previous caveat concerning the absence of evidence, this is a strong indication that by this period in history Carl Wark had ceased to have any importance.

Looking to the Future

An archaeological challenge: what can be done to solve the mystery?

We have seen that the once accepted portrayal of Carl Wark as an Iron Age period hillfort is highly speculative (although still just as likely as any other period) and in particular that this mysterious monument to the past may well have had peaceful origins as a ritual enclosure. If that were the case, then a second phase of construction seems to have occurred which adapted it from a symbolic construction into a defensive one. Yet equally possible was the notion that Carl Wark was built in a single phase as a fortress - either to resist the Roman occupation, or to fight off a new wave of oppressors, perhaps during the later fifth or sixth centuries, but like so much about Carl Wark this remains pure speculation. Nor is their any evidence that Carl Wark was ever occupied in the sense of having houses or buildings for storage, although we do know that the area surrounding Carl Wark has been inhabited since at least the Mesolithic period.

In trying to unravel the mystery particular attention has to be paid to Carl Wark's most imposing features, its western stone rampart and its entrance. Their stone and turf construction tend to indicate that they were constructed after the introduction of this technique to Britain by the Roman army. That theory is based on very firm assertions by C. M. Piggott and if accepted, favours a Dark Age date for the construction.

Unfortunately Piggott's argument is tenuous, to say the least, given that many Iron Age hillforts were built using turf, albeit not stone faced. Ramparts have been found with turf cores covered in soil thrown up as the adjacent defensive ditch was dug out. Even the Roman marching camps used turf and soil, with the turf some times being used to clad the more unstable soil. Simple though it may seem, Trustram's hypothesis that Carl Wark's very early builders independently 'invented' the idea of a defensive stone wall out of necessity has a lot to offer.

What is probably even more detrimental to Piggott's views about the use of turf at Carl Wark is that we do not know for certain the stone rampart is backed by turf rather than soil. Only the lack of a ditch (the very point underpinning Trustram's hypothesis) from which soil has been removed can support his theory until such times as an excavation determines the true situation.

Carl Wark was critically located so that it may well have played a role in the internecine struggles of the Celtic tribes or later, between the Saxon kingdoms of Mercia and Northumbria. Or as its very last act of defiance, Carl Wark could even have been a place of Anglian resistance to Danish invaders.

Ideally then, what is required to complete these explanations for Carl Wark's existence? Whilst a great deal of research into the history of Carl Wark and the surrounding region has been achieved from written records, historical accounts and site visits, further scientific study and especially, excavation, is needed if the questions which remain are to be answered.

The first stage of an archaeological investigation would involve carrying out a geophysical survey, a procedure which has become familiar to viewers of Channel Four's excellent 'Time Team' series.

This should reveal the existence of any subsurface irregularities which could indicate the presence of buildings, pits or other anomalies caused by human activity. Then, again as seen so often in a Time Team investigation, the geophysical survey would be followed by trial excavations. A decision would then have to be made on whether full scale excavation was feasible - not such a straightforward matter bearing in mind the financial and time constraints imposed on this type of work and the need to recruit suitably skilled workers. The work is nowhere near finished when a 'dig' ends of course. Post excavation work such as identifying, preserving and recording finds, not to mention writing and publishing an account for other interested parties, can take many years.

Until the day an excavation at Carl Wark becomes a reality, we can only speculate on the questions concerning its origins. If you have never visited the monument, why not go and see what you can make of it yourself? And even if you have been before, then hopefully, after reading this short account, another visit will enable you to more fully appreciate the mystery of Carl Wark.

Fortress or folly? The choice is yours.

Chronology

Archaeologists use specific terms for particular periods of the past. You may not be familiar with all of these, so to help you they are listed below, together with their approximate dates. Of course there was no sudden, noticeable change from one period to another. Change was immensely slower than it is today and the transition from one phase to another took place over very long periods and at various times in different parts of Britain, and of course in the rest of the world. For example, while people in Britain had still to discover metalworking, there were already advanced, literate societies in Syria, at Mohenjodaro in Pakistan, and of course in Egypt.

Period:	Dates:
Palaeolithic	500,000 - 8,300 BC (Subdivided into Lower, Middle and Upper)
Mesolithic	8,300 - 3,500 BC
Neolithic	3,500 - 1,800 BC
Bronze Age	1,800 - 800 BC
Iron Age	800 BC - AD 43
Romano-British	AD 43 - 410
Anglian and Danish	AD 410 - 1068
Medieval	AD 1068 - 1550
Post Medieval	AD 1550 onwards

Suggested Reading

ADDY, S. O. *The Hall of Waltheof*, Townsend & Son: Sheffield, 1893 (Limited Edition)

ANDERSON, J. J. *Roman Derbyshire: The Roman Colonisation of Derbyshire*, Derbyshire Heritage: Derby, 1986.

ASTON, M. *Interpreting the Landscape*, Batsford: London,1992.

BAHN, P. (Ed) *Collins Dictionary of Archaeology*, Harper Collins: Glasgow, 1992.

BARKER, P. *Techniques of Archaeological Excavation*, Batsford: London, 1982.

BARNATT, J. & SMITH, K. *The Peak District: Landscapes Through Time*, English Heritage: London, 1997.

BLAIR, P. H. *An Introduction to Anglo-Saxon England, (2nd. edition)*, Cambridge University Press, 1988.

BRAMWELL, D. *Archaeology in the Peak District*, Moorland: Stafford, 1973.

BRANIGAN, K. (Ed.) *Rome and the Brigantes: The Impact of Rome on Northern England*, University of Sheffield, 1980.

BUTTERWORTH, A. & LEWIS, G. D. *Prehistoric and Roman Times in the Sheffield Area*, Sheffield City Museums, 1978.

CAMERON, K. *The Place Names of Derbyshire*, Cambridge University Press, 1959.

COLLINGWOOD, R. G. & MYRES, J. N. L. *Roman Britain and the English Settlements*, Oxford University Press: London, 1968.

COOMBS, D. G. & THOMPSON, F. H. *Excavation of the Hillfort of Mam Tor, 1965-69*, Derbyshire Archaeological Journal No. 49, 1979.

CUNLIFFE, B. & POOLE, C. *Danebury: An Iron Age Hillfort in Hampshire Vol. 4*, 1988, CBA Res. Rep. 73.

CUNLIFFE, B. *Danebury: An Iron Age Hillfort in Hampshire*, CBA Res. Rep. 52, 1984.
CUNLIFFE, B. *Iron Age Britain,* Batsford: London, 1995.
DARVILL, T. *Prehistoric Britain,* Batsford: London, 1993.
EKWALL, E. *The Concise Oxford Dictionary of English Place-Names, 4th Edition,* 1960.
FIRTH, J. B. *Highways and Byways in Derbyshire,* Macmillan & Co.: London, 1905.
GOULD, I. C. *Carl's Wark,* Derbyshire Archaeological Journal No. 25, 1903, pp 175-180.
HALL, S. T. *The Peak and the Plain: Scenes in Woodland, Field & Mountain,* Houlston & Stoneman: London, 1853.
HARRIS, H. *Industrial Archaeology of the Peak District,* David and Charles, 1971.
HART, C. R. *The North Derbyshire Archaeological Survey,* North Derbyshire Archaeological Trust, 1981.
LAING, J. & LAING, L. *The Origins of Britain,* Granada: London, 1982.
LEYLAND, J. *The Peak of Derbyshire: Its Scenery and Antiquities,* Seeley & Co.: London, 1891.
MUSSON, C. *The Breiddin Hillfort: A Later Prehistoric Settlement in the Welsh Marches,* 1991, Council for British Archaeology Research Report 76: London.
ORDNANCE SURVEY. *Ancient Britain,* 1990, Ordnance Survey: Southampton.
PIGGOTT, C. M. *Carl Wark: A Hillfort In Derbyshire,* Antiquity No. 25, 1951, Notes and News, pp. 210 212.
RENFREW, C. (Ed) *British Prehistory: A New Outline,* Duckworth: London, 1980.
RENFREW, C. & BAHN, P. *Archaeology: Theories, Methods and Practice,* Thames & Hudson: London, 1991.
REYNOLDS, P. J. *Iron Age Farm: The Butser Experiment,* British Museum: London, 1979.